EMPLOYE

to

21

VOLUNTARY

BENEFITS

Your Employees Will LOVE!

(And LOVE You For Offering)

DONNA JOSEPH

PETE TOBIASON

Bayne & Prospect Books

Thank you for buying this Book

Published by Bayne & Prospect Books
an imprint of
Rhodes-Joseph & Tobiason Advisors

To receive special offers,
bonus content and news about employee
benefits
and our latest books, sign up for our
newsletter at

bit.ly/RJTANews
(this address is case sensitive)

Or visit us online to sign up at

www.RJTAdvisors.com

Reader Praise for

Making Voluntary WORKPLACE BENEFITS A Valued Feature of Every Employer's Benefits Program

by
Donna Joseph and Pete Tobiason

"Excellent"
****

"A wonderful job; it will help current and future practitioners."
****

"Thumbs up"
****

"A great resource"
****

"A very useful tool"

Copyright

Published by Bayne & Prospect Books, an imprint of
Rhodes-Joseph & Tobiason Advisors, LLC,
www.RJTAdvisors.com
First eBook edition: July, 2015
First print edition: January, 2016

You can find Donna Joseph and Pete Tobiason online at
www.RJTAdvisors.com   and
www.GrowYourBenefitsCareer.com

Twitter
Follow Donna @BenefitsCoach
Follow Pete   @PeteRJTA

ISBN # (print edition) 978-0-9826204-4-1

permission of both the copyright owners and the publisher of this book.

Table of Contents

—

Preface

Even the very best HR and Benefits professionals like you are overwhelmed by the variety of new benefits product designs, by ever-changing government rules (think ACA or HIPAA) and by the increasingly complex and often burdensome challenges of administration. Each day you wonder what benefits crisis story will go viral or be reported on CNBC or on page one of the Wall Street Journal – stories that will prompt calls and emails from your management and your employees. And then, what new discussions and challenges follow?

Let's face it. Your life is complex enough when everything is running smoothly without introducing anything new or different into your programs.

Challenges and opportunities are coming at you from all directions. Vendors offering innovative programs. Brokers and consultants presenting new ideas and solutions. Will Private Exchanges deliver on the promise to simplify and improve your benefits program?

You care about your employees. You ask yourself – what can I do to make a difference in their lives?

HR and Benefits Pros have the power to help employees. To change things. To make a difference.

Before we get started, we want to tell you why we wrote this book. We are passionate about employee benefits and how they can help employees meet life needs. We've had the privilege of managing employee benefits for a very complex organization. And we've also been fortunate to coach people working in employee benefits, providing them independent and practical strategies when they need it.

We wrote this book to give you ideas and strategies for achieving specific and measurable long-lasting results, by presenting the story of Voluntary Benefits in one convenient place. We want to equip you with information, strategies, and key action steps to give you new perspectives and resources for discussions with your brokers/consultants and product providers, your top management and your employees.

Just imagine how your benefits program can meet the needs of your diverse and multi-generation workforce, while helping your company hire and retain workers who are not distracted during work, and so are more productive.

This Employer's Quick Guide is about how to go from where you are today to where you want your program to be. You'll get an overview of today's Voluntary Benefits and tools that can help you move your program forward.

We all know a little (or a lot) about Voluntary Benefits. (These are also sometimes called Worksite, Ancillary or Supplemental Benefits.) They're part of many employers' benefits program. But why aren't they part of every employee benefits program? And why do some employers only offer one or two Voluntary Benefits?

We are convinced that the value of Voluntary Benefits to employees is underestimated by some employers. We know that employees can be distracted at work by concerns that can be addressed by Voluntary Benefits – that these benefits can provide the resources employees need to help them deal with issues that are distracting them, allowing them to remain focused on their work

Offering Voluntary Benefits can improve your employees' perceptions of your company. They can turn your employees into corporate fans who promote your company's brand, not only to customers, but as well to prospective employees. Word of mouth is a powerful tool. You want your employees to tell their friends the value they get from your company!

The basics of Voluntary Benefits. Voluntary Benefits are employee paid plans offered as part of employee benefits programs and are an increasingly important feature of these programs. They fill benefits program gaps. They supplement your core benefits. And they can enhance your program at minimal costs to your company.

For your employees, they can offer a wide choice of alternatives to meet their needs. The choices have been vetted by a trusted source – you! Employees don't have to "shop" for the protections they need and they can pay through convenient payroll deductions.

Voluntary Benefits can help employees feel like a work life balance is attainable – and help their well-being. And even if the employee doesn't choose the benefit, the mere fact that Voluntary Benefits are made available can make employees feel valued and cared for.

Employees whose life needs are met by Voluntary Benefits will be less distracted when those needs show up.

How did we choose the 21 Voluntary Benefits from the variety available in the market today? While the number and categories of Voluntary Benefits grows almost daily, we decided to focus our Quick Guide on 21 Voluntary Benefits that we see being widely adopted by employers like you.

Now let's get started with 21 Voluntary Benefits your employees will love and love you for offering.

Chapter 1

Introduction

The Question. Our Quick Guide answers the question we so often hear from employers – what Voluntary Benefits should I offer my employees?

The Answer At a Glance. We like to say that for both employers and employees, "Voluntary Benefits are the Benefits You Choose™".

In Part 1, we identify and explain 21 Voluntary Benefits that address the life needs of your employees. In Part 2 we highlight key processes and concepts to help you achieve Voluntary Benefits success. In Part 3 we share a checklist of 10 quick steps to help you meet your Voluntary Benefits goals.

Voluntary Benefits are paid for by employees and sometimes paid for in part by their employer. By including a wide range of Voluntary Benefits in your benefits program, you help employees meet many of their life needs in a cost effective and convenient way, increase employee satisfaction and loyalty and improve workforce productivity.

Voluntary Benefits complement and coordinate with your core benefits for health, retirement and financial protection. A comprehensive menu of Voluntary Benefits rounds out your benefits program and offers employees valuable resources to meet life needs not being met by core benefits. At the same time, they enhance your ability to attract and retain valuable talent. Voluntary Benefits can also help your company control benefits costs while offering new choices to employees. Through these employer facilitated programs, employees gain access to valuable protection and services, usually at favorable rates, and they pay through convenient payroll deductions.

Employee benefits are vital tools, helping employees meet their life needs and those of their families. Voluntary Benefits add value, and strengthen your total benefits program. Know the choices that are available in today's market. If your employees have a need that isn't being met by your current benefits program, consider adding Voluntary Benefits. These are benefits employees love – and will love you for offering!

The Communication Challenge. Communication and education are key to your employees' understanding and appreciating the value of your benefits program. Communication is central to Voluntary Benefits success, as we demonstrate in Part 2. And throughout this guide we note unique communication challenges associated with specific Voluntary Benefits.

The Global Connection. Employee life needs met by Voluntary Benefits are not unique to any one country. Benefits paid for by employee contributions are growing in popularity not only in the U.S. but globally as well. This growth is an acknowledgement that neither employers nor governments can afford to provide benefits that meet every life need. For employers with employees working outside the U.S., use this guide to help analyze employee paid benefits to enhance your local benefits program and make yours a business of choice wherever you do business throughout the world.

How To Use This Guide. Evaluate your current benefits program. What life needs does your program meet? What life needs aren't being met? What do your employees need to protect themselves and their families? What are you hearing from new hires and during the interview process? Find out what's available in today's Voluntary Benefits marketplace that your employees may want. Use this guide to help you strategically plan your benefits program and take action now!

Keep this Guide for Future Reference. Remember to review this guide and all your benefits plans periodically as part of your strategic benefits planning.

PART 1

21 Voluntary Employee Benefits

Voluntary Employee Benefits - What to Look For. The variety of Voluntary Benefits grows every day. To appreciate the potential for Voluntary Benefits, it's helpful to think in terms of the broad categories of life needs that we all have. Voluntary Benefits address health and wellness, financial and retirement protection, and an expanding list of employees' everyday life needs.

An important note on financial well-being. While these life needs categories contribute to better understanding of the role Voluntary Benefits play in employees' lives, all these benefits ultimately support employees' financial wellness. Voluntary Benefits fill gaps in your core benefits program. They provide protection from the impact of unexpected life events. They help employees protect their financial readiness for retirement. And they help employees understand and take control of their financial life.

Here are 21 Voluntary Benefits that together meet a wide variety of vital life needs.

Chapter 2

Health and Wellness

To help meet the health needs of your employees, look at critical illness, dental care, vision and other health and wellness related Voluntary Benefits. These plans can meet employees' life needs by helping them pay for costs not met by your company's traditional health care plans. Many of these programs now include attractive wellness features for employees and family members.

Here are the first eight of the 21 Voluntary Benefits your employees will love:

1. **Critical Illness**
2. **Dental**
3. **Vision**
4. **Hearing**
5. **Health Wellness**
6. **Hospitalization**
7. **Accident**
8. **Telemedicine**

Voluntary Critical Illness Insurance

Critical Illness plans help pay for extra expenses when your employees become critically ill or severely injured. The non-medical expenses employees may face include travel, child care, special equipment for care at home and lost wages of the caregiver.

Critical Illness plans (also called specified disease or cancer insurance) are often one of the first Voluntary Benefits offered by employers. Critical Illness insurance is widely publicized through direct-to-consumer advertising. The benefit provides cash when it's needed most. It's a concept that's readily understood by employees and you can build on this foundation of product familiarity when introducing Critical Illness plans to your employees.

Today's employees are keenly aware of the extra costs that occur when they or a family member have a major illness. Critical Illness insurance is a visible benefit in the workplace when the payment is made, and it's often a topic of favorable conversation among employees.

For employers that offer a high deductible health plan – and for those who use a defined contribution approach to their benefits - Critical Illness insurance can be an important enhancement to their benefits program. It offers valuable financial protection for employees and their families, helping fill gaps in medical plan designs. Critical Illness benefits can also be used to pay for expenses such as deductibles, copayments or experimental procedures not covered under the medical plan.

With a Critical Illness policy in place, employees will be less distracted and financially stressed by the cost of medical and personal expenses while they're dealing with these serious illnesses.

Critical Illness insurance pays a lump sum cash benefit directly to the employee if they're diagnosed with one of the major illnesses covered under the plan. Some examples are heart attacks, cancer and strokes.

The benefit payment can be used for any purpose. It's not reimbursement to the health care provider for services. It's not considered health insurance. It's money to be used by employees as they choose.

Coverage can be either on a standalone basis with simplified, quick claims handling or coordinated with core medical plans. When offered by the same insurance carrier/provider as the medical plan, the employee can have a seamless experience (including claims processing).

Promotion and advertising for these plans often highlight expenses that are not medical in nature, that an employee has when they're experiencing major illness - like travel, child care and income replacement.

Marketing messages may also point to using the cash payment for other expenses not specifically related to the illness, such as mortgage payments, rent or utility bills.

When you evaluate these plans, be sure to consider the illnesses covered and the limitations. As with all benefits plans, you want employees to have a realistic expectation of what the coverage will provide and what it won't. Be sure the provider's enrollment communication is clear and complete.

Voluntary Dental Care

Dental Care benefits plans are often part of an employer's core benefits program. However, with employers reexamining their health related benefits strategy and costs, offering dental benefits on a fully employee paid basis is becoming more common. Despite the shift from employer support to a Voluntary Benefit, dental coverage remains an integral part of health care benefits.

Some insured dental plans restrict benefits to a network of providers only, while others include both network and out-of-network benefits. Plans may have a deductible and co-insurance. Non-insured plans feature a discount from participating dentists, and the employee pays the dentist directly.

Dental Care benefits may be offered through medical plan insurers. Dental plans are also offered by standalone providers and insurers that are not in the medical plan market.

Dental plans commonly cover preventive services such as routine exams and cleanings, often at a higher level of coverage than other services, including a waiver of any plan deductible. Other services – often categorized as "basic" and "major" – are included at differing coverage levels. Annual limits on the amount of benefits that are paid are common; some plans have lifetime limits as well. Limited coverage for orthodontia treatment is available in many plans. Be sure to check the benefits levels, included services and plan deductibles and copays when comparing products.

Dental plans provide an important part of an employer's wellness initiatives by encouraging preventive dental care, and prompt attention to dental issues.

Voluntary Vision Care

Vision Care benefits help pay for the cost of glasses, contact lenses and eye exams, eye care typically not covered by medical plans.

Employees like Vision Care because every day health expenses that they're likely to experience are covered. They like having their family covered for regular eye exams and getting help to pay for glasses and contacts.

Some Vision Care plans specify a network of opticians and ophthalmologists. Others also cover services outside a network - from any licensed provider - but with higher out-of-pocket costs. Plan benefits may be used at local retail providers as well as national eyewear chains.

Some vision plans include coverage for laser vision correction surgery along with decision support resources, which help employees considering the Lasik alternative.

Although paid for by your employees, Vision Care is appreciated as part of your wellness initiatives. And by encouraging regular eye exams, vision benefits contribute to improved employee productivity.

A note about Vision Care and the Affordable Care Act. The ACA considers vision care for children an Essential Health Benefit. Accordingly you'll find that health plans now include eye exams and eyewear for children. Voluntary Vision Care is an attractive addition to your benefits program, as it expands eye exams, glasses and contact lenses coverage to the whole family.

Voluntary Hearing Care

Hearing benefits help make the cost of hearing testing and devices more affordable at a time of growing need for hearing assistance.

Most medical plans don't cover hearing devices, or if they do, the benefits are very limited. Yet employees and family members can experience significant hearing loss – children first diagnosed at a young age, older adults with age related hearing loss and, increasingly, millennials and others exposed to excessive noise using headphones and attending rock concerts.

Employees value hearing benefits because they provide help for testing, education and hearing aids when it's needed. Hearing benefits are typically designed as discounts for the services of network audiologists, ENT physicians and hearing aid providers. Services can include screenings, consultations, cleanings and battery replacements.

Hearing loss can significantly impact workplace productivity and communication as well as overall quality of life. Hearing benefits are another important part of your wellness initiatives.

Some hearing care programs are offered as discounts under an employer's health plan, or as part of another Voluntary Benefits plan such as vision care. Be sure to check your current plans, and if this benefit is already available to your employees, communicate it as part of your total benefits program.

Voluntary Health Wellness

Health Wellness benefits resemble traditional wellness programs that are fully provided for by employers but instead, as a voluntary plan, are paid for by your employees.

Wellness is center stage in the growing movement to improve employee health. Employers add wellness features to health plans and offer wellness programs to help employees and their families change unhealthy behaviors. Wellness initiatives may provide access to health related information and offer tools to develop personal wellness plans. Awareness of the need for wellness is growing through media and education, and employees look to their employer for health information, resources, and direction.

Offering a wellness program as a voluntary benefit - which is not incentive or penalty driven, but paid for by the employee - can enhance your wellness initiatives, adding valuable features to your existing wellness programs for your employees and their family members. And employee commitment to wellness may be greater when the employee pays.

These programs can range from discounted memberships at the local Y or fitness centers, employee elected health risk assessments, health screenings and access to smoking cessation, obesity/weight management, nutrition, wellness coaching and stress reduction programs (think meditation and yoga) at favorable group rates. They can also include fitness and health apps and health related wearables.

While many of today's wellness programs are paid for by employers, there are significant numbers of businesses that aren't in a position to financially support wellness offerings. Introducing Voluntary Wellness benefits can be a meaningful new alternative for employers who care about the health and wellness of employees and their families but who cannot afford employer-subsidized wellness offerings.

Strategically positioned in your benefits program as a Voluntary Benefit, employee paid wellness programs provide your employees access to a wide menu of wellness services and resources not otherwise available to them.

Employee loyalty increases as they recognize that their company is concerned with their well-being. Productivity increases as employees use wellness tools to help address stress and other life issues. And healthier employee behavior can help reduce your health plan costs.

Voluntary Hospitalization Insurance

Hospitalization Insurance complements your health plan, paying a cash benefit for individuals who are admitted to a hospital. These types of plans are also known as hospital indemnity plans or supplemental group hospital indemnity insurance.

Benefits can be used for any purpose. Often employees use the cash payment for out-of-pocket medical expenses or for personal expenses such as child care, transportation or rent.

Voluntary Hospitalization plans typically pay lump sum benefits for each hospital confinement or a daily benefit for each day the person is an inpatient. Some plans feature both types of payments. Additional benefits may be paid for intensive care confinements, emergency room treatment or rehabilitation facilities.

Hospitalization Insurance supplements existing medical coverage and helps close the gaps associated with high deductible plans.

As with all benefits, its important that employees are aware of waiting periods, pre-existing condition limitations and portability provisions.

Voluntary Accident Insurance

Accident insurance provides benefits that are in addition to those generally covered under health plans.

It's a fixed cash benefit amount paid to the employee when a serious accidental injury occurs. Generally plans provide payments for qualified accidents ranging from broken bones or sprains to major events.

Similar to critical illness, accident plans help fill gaps in high deductible health plans.

Voluntary Accident insurance plans provide limited coverage - generally a schedule of payments for covered accidental injuries. Benefits can be paid to the insured and can help employees pay out-of-pocket medical expenses or cover ongoing costs such as mortgages and rent. Some plan designs reimburse out-of-pocket medical expenses up to a maximum benefit.

A major communication challenge for this benefit is helping employees understand that the plan is designed to cover only specified accidents substantiated by medical records during the claim process.

Voluntary Telemedicine

Telemedicine features phone or on-line access to networks of physicians as an alternative to doctor visits. Employees get information, or specific help diagnosing conditions and symptoms without actually visiting a doctor.

Employees can discuss routine medical conditions with physicians and explore treatment options. Many common conditions can be diagnosed via phone and the doctor can send a prescription to a pharmacy if needed. Conditions commonly treated are colds, flus, allergies and infections.

Telemedicine doesn't replace the services of a primary care physician, but gives employees access to a physician at any time. If telemedicine services are not offered under your health plan, employees may want to purchase 24/7 access to a medical professional.

When offered as a Voluntary Benefit, employees pay a monthly fee for access to the services, often without any additional charge for copays, deductibles or a charge for the call.

Major employers and health plans are increasingly including telemedicine in their programs, and it's expected that these services will be offered more widely in the next few years. If your health plan already includes these services, be sure to promote them.

Whether offered through your health plan or as a Voluntary Benefit, telemedicine is expected to help reduce your health plan costs by eliminating unnecessary office and ER visits. If telemedicine is not part of your health plan, consider offering it as a Voluntary Benefit to enhance your total health and wellness program.

Chapter 3

Financial Protection

When an unexpected financial catastrophe strikes, it can severely impact your employees' ability to protect their families and safeguard their assets for retirement. Financial protection Voluntary Benefits answer this life need. Life insurance and disability insurance provide financial support to employees and their families in times of distress. Long term care becomes more necessary for employees as longevity increases and more individuals need assistance as they age.

Here are the four financial protection insurance products included in our 21 Voluntary Benefits:

9.	**Life Insurance**
10.	**Short Term Disability**
11.	**Long Term Disability**
12.	**Long Term Care**

Voluntary Life Insurance

Life insurance helps employees fine-tune their financial protection. Life and accident insurance ("AD&D") help assure that an employee's family will be able to keep their home and pay for education.

Employers have long recognized that all employees should have a minimum level of life insurance. Typically this valuable benefit is referred to as basic coverage, often offered as a fixed amount of coverage or an amount related to pay.

When you look at voluntary life insurance plans (often called "supplemental life insurance"), you see an effective model integrating company provided and employee paid benefits. Employees get both basic protection and the flexibility to adjust their benefits coverage to meet their individual needs.

A well recognized principle of financial planning is that life insurance needs vary by life stage and family circumstances. To accommodate this variety of life needs, employers offer employees the ability to purchase additional life insurance, taking advantage of favorable group rates and limited or no underwriting requirements. In many plans, employees are able to purchase additional amounts of insurance coverage in salary related increments; multiples of 5 to 8 times pay are not uncommon.

Coverage is not limited to employees. Many plans provide the option to purchase life insurance for spouses and partners as well as for dependent children. These plans recognize the significant financial impact of any loss of life on an employee and their family members.

The portability of supplemental life insurance is a very valuable feature for employees, because as individuals age, their ability to become insured can be limited by medical conditions.

When comparing supplemental life insurance plans, you'll find a wide choice of products and insurers. The most common form of supplemental life insurance is term life, where premiums increase as an individual ages. Often voluntary supplemental life insurance is combined with an optional cash accumulation vehicle, in a financially attractive universal life product.

Voluntary Disability Protection

Disability insurance protects future income during working years, helping employees meet everyday expenses when they can't work. It's a key protection from financial catastrophe during their career. Experiencing a period of not being able to work because of a disability is more likely than collecting on life insurance during the working years.

Disability coverage on a voluntary basis addresses both short and long term periods of disability. It typically allows an employee to choose the portion of their income that will be protected, the waiting period that they can cover with their own resources before benefits commence, and the length of time for which disability benefits will be provided.

As with life insurance, the portability feature of voluntary short and long term disability plans is especially valuable to employees who may not be able to qualify in the future for similar coverage.

When taken together, these plans can provide a needed income stream which protects the employee's home, retirement savings and other personal assets.

Voluntary Short Term Disability insurance plans replace income – either partially or fully – for temporary illnesses or injuries when your employees cannot work for a short period of time. Many companies provide limited income continuation for a period of days or weeks, often under sick pay or paid time off policies. Voluntary Short Term Disability starts to pay benefits after the company provided payments end.

It's not uncommon to find short term coverage provided as part of an employer's core, company paid benefits. However, some businesses do not offer this coverage, or may offer basic coverage at a lower benefit. Voluntary Short Term Disability helps close this coverage gap.

Short term disability insurance replaces a percentage of income for a defined period of time. Variable waiting periods and benefit payment periods are options. With a voluntary program, employees can choose their benefit replacement amount and period of coverage.

Voluntary Long Term Disability insurance plans replace income for longer periods of time. Waiting (or elimination) periods, before benefits can begin, are commonly 3 or 6 months. Benefits under long term plans can continue for lengthy periods, sometimes up to age 65, the expected retirement age for most employees.

Long Term Disability provides retirement protection so that employees don't have to draw down their savings or retirement accounts.

With Voluntary Long Term Disability, employees have the opportunity to buy protection if they are unable to work for a long period of time due to serious illness or injury and to tailor the coverage to meet their personal needs. For some employees, Voluntary Long Term Disability may be the only disability benefit offered at work. For others, a voluntary program gives them the opportunity to purchase benefits that are higher than the amounts available under their employer's core plan.

Voluntary Long Term Care Insurance

Long Term Care insurance protects assets both before and after retirement by helping meet expenses of nursing home or home health care that are not covered under medical plans or Medicare.

Long Term Care protection fills a critical gap in benefits coverage. More than ever, employees are aware of the challenges facing the aging population, and the high costs of obtaining needed assistance.

These plans cover nursing home services and home health care assistance - services needed for people who are unable to care for themselves. These are individuals with chronic illnesses or disabilities that prevent them from performing simple activities without assistance. Most of the expenses covered under these plans are not covered under employer sponsored medical plans, public health care exchange plans or Medicare.

A major concern to employees is the significant cost of Long Term Care insurance premiums. Carriers are addressing this concern by developing hybrid products that combine long term care benefits with other plans such as life insurance and critical illness insurance.

Long Term Care is an especially complex insurance product. As such, it illustrates a key challenge of Voluntary Benefits plans. The enrollment method used for each category of Voluntary Benefits must be appropriate to the complexity and other special characteristics of the plans. In the case of Long Term Care plans, specialists who are skilled in the communication of these plans work with employers to formulate enrollment and implementation strategies tailored to their workforce.

Chapter 4

Everyday Financial Life Needs

There's a growing category of Voluntary Benefits that help employees with everyday financial life needs. Identity theft protection, auto and home insurance, legal services and pet protection/insurance are popular Voluntary Benefits plans because they help employees purchase these protections in a cost effective, convenient way.

Our 21 Voluntary Benefits include six Voluntary Benefits that help with everyday financial life needs.

13.	**Legal Services**
14.	**Identity Theft Protection**
15.	**Auto Insurance**
16.	**Home Insurance**
17.	**Pet Protection/Insurance**
18.	**Child and Elder Care**

Voluntary Legal Services Plans

Many employees do not have an existing relationship with a lawyer but may experience an unexpected, urgent need for legal advice. Legal Services plans help employees engage the services of an attorney.

Employees gain access to a lawyer at favorable cost. These plans are attractive as a way for employees to have available what would otherwise be relatively expensive, and often difficult to locate, services.

Employees have access to help with a variety of legal issues and events – including preparing and updating wills, home purchase, apartment rental, buying a car, adoption, divorce, tax issues, retirement planning and bankruptcy. Employees can get help preparing powers of attorney and health care proxies and preparing and reviewing legal contracts and documents.

Offered as a Voluntary Benefit with favorable group rated contributions, Legal Services plans attract the interest of employees of all generations.

Legal Services plans make it easier for employees to locate an attorney when help is needed. Participation in the plan gives employees the ability to have an attorney on their side, reducing distraction from the worry and financial impact of the legal issues that they're facing.

A variety of design models are available in the marketplace. Some are fully insured; some designs offer credentialed attorney networks that are paid in full for covered events while other designs have copays like an indemnity health plan. Others offer discounts on legal services.

Some plans require that you use a network provider; others provide in-network and out-of-network levels of benefits. Many offer resources such as legal information and sample documents.

The monthly premium cost for each design depends on the type and level of service. As is the case with other Voluntary Benefits, the cost paid by your employees is an important planning and design consideration. Whenever you consider a new Voluntary Benefit, you'll want to evaluate the balance of features vs. affordability that's most appropriate for your employee population.

Voluntary Identity Theft Protection

Identity theft is one of the most frequently encountered financial risks faced today. Stolen identity can directly threaten your employees. Credit card and bank accounts can be compromised. Year after year identity theft is at the top of the FTC's list of consumer concerns.

With newly discovered security breaches involving tens of millions of customers being reported almost every day, it's becoming more likely that some of your employees will face the severe distraction of reconstructing their credit. Employees recognize the need for identity theft protection and appreciate your making these plans available to them through the workplace

Membership in an identity theft protection program helps employees monitor their credit, and if their identity is compromised, the program helps them through the difficult reconstruction process and allows them to refocus on their work.

Identity theft protection programs offer both credit protection and credit restoration services. Some plans feature credit monitoring services which track credit reports and notify a participant when an inquiry is made. Optional services may be offered that help employees rebuild their damaged financial identity. Some plans also include protection for health data to combat health insurance fraud.

Other services may include ID theft insurance to cover the costs of restoring identity, child identity monitoring services, internet surveillance and lost wallet services.

Identity theft protection may be structured as a feature that's included in a legal services plan, or it may be a standalone product.

Voluntary Auto Insurance and Home Insurance

Employees find Auto and Home Insurance appealing and relevant to their personal lives.

Most employees already have these insurance plans on their own. States require auto insurance for anyone who owns or leases a car. Auto insurance can also provide insurance for other vehicles such as motorcycles, RVs and boats.

Most employees also want to have home insurance to insure the value of their home and their personal belongings, and mortgage lenders generally require this coverage. And there are policies designed to meet specific needs of employees that rent apartments or condominiums.

Voluntary Auto and Home Insurance benefits offer the convenience of payroll deductions together with discounted rates.

Auto and home plans are not limited to your annual enrollment cycle. Employees have different renewal dates for their existing policies. At any time during the year, they may buy a new home, move to a new rental residence, or buy or lease a new car. Auto and home insurers provide communication support and enrollment opportunities throughout the year for their voluntary programs.

Voluntary Pet Protection/Insurance

For employers who currently do not offer Voluntary Benefits or offer a limited Voluntary Benefits menu, pet protection (insurance or discounts) is an ideal first or next offering as a Voluntary Benefit. Many of your employees have pets. Even those who don't have pets will appreciate the employer who recognizes the needs of their "pet parent" colleagues.

Americans spend billions of dollars each year on their pets' health. Pet protection addresses a significant financial need for those with pets. Employees care about their pets and this coverage can reduce employee distraction and financial concerns. The pet protection market is well developed and health benefits for pets are likely known to your employees through previous employment or through friends and colleagues.

Employees get attractive rates and payroll convenience for pet insurance through employer based programs.

There are two popular design models of pet protection; both can cover accidents, illnesses and pet wellness.

Pet health insurance resembles health insurance for humans. Employees pay a monthly premium and get reimbursed for veterinary services when their pets need care. Designs can include deductibles (annual or per occurrence), copays, annual or lifetime limits, different levels of reimbursement, schedules of benefit payments, and pre-existing condition exclusions and limitations.

Pet protection discount programs offer employees discounts at participating veterinarians and other providers.

Insurance and discount benefits are typically available for cats and dogs. For other pets, and for some special breeds, coverage may be available as an option.

Voluntary Child and Elder Care Benefits

Child and Elder care services are important Voluntary Benefits for those employees whose family circumstances call for them.

Finding adequate child care and adult/senior care is becoming more and more challenging. An employee trying to balance job demands with the responsibility for the care of another person may be very distracted and unable to concentrate on work. They may be at work physically but pre-occupied trying to line up adequate care. Or they may have to handle the situation themselves and be absent.

In the past, employers have focused on employees' needs for child care, and some employers have arrangements with local day care centers for children. But the growing responsibilities that baby boomers and others have for their aging parents and other family members often have not been addressed.

Today, there are on-line services with membership fees that are available to help employees find quality care on a regular basis or for back-up care. Employers can add membership to these on-line services to their menu of Voluntary Benefits, enabling employees to use payroll deductions to pay for their membership fee.

Employees who enroll in the program will have help managing their child/senior care issues and can be more productive at work.

In addition to child and elder care, some care companies also offer services for taking care of pets, tutoring, and housekeeping services.

Chapter 5

Financial Wellness

Wellness, by which we mean that employees and their families experience health, security and well-being rather than ills and accompanying stress, today applies not only to physical wellness but also to financial wellness.

Employers are seeing their employees stressed by overwhelming financial issues – such as credit problems, student loans and debt management. They are recognizing that improving their employees' financial security, financial health and financial well-being is critical to reducing "presenteeism" (when an employee is physically present at work but not focused) and increasing workplace productivity.

Employers who want to encourage employee financial wellness but who have exhausted their employee benefits budget are looking to financial wellness programs that can be offered as Voluntary Benefits. These programs can help, offering employees financial education and counseling, debt and credit counseling and responsible product purchasing.

The final three of our 21 Voluntary Benefits support financial wellness:

Voluntary Financial Education and Counseling / Debt and Credit Counseling

Employers understand that, for their employees to be more fully productive at work, the stresses of financial challenges need to be addressed. Like health wellness, improving employees' financial wellness is a goal for employers who are concerned about these financial stresses and the impact they have on work.

The goal of these education and counseling programs is to enhance financial literacy so that employees are better able to manage their financial lives and therefore are less distracted and more productive at work.

Voluntary Financial Education and Counseling programs help employees plan and budget. These programs go beyond traditional retirement planning programs, helping employees manage their finances throughout their working career. While some employers pay for financial education for all employees, others make it available on a voluntary basis.

Employees who are overwhelmed with financial needs and opportunities want to understand credit basics, credit reports, investing, insurance, mortgages, college financing and more. They want to be sure their spending is appropriate for their income. They want to budget effectively.

Employees want to become financially literate. They know they need to take responsibility and use tools to make wise financial decisions for themselves and their families. And they need financial information appropriate to the different stages of their lives. They may be buying or selling a home. They may be looking at college or higher education for their children or themselves. Financial literacy enables them to analyze and understand their finances and their opportunities.

A voluntary, employee-paid financial education and counseling program can provide the tools that employees want and need. Programs may offer on-line education, apps for mobile devices, print material and one-on-one phone counseling. Employees can choose the level and format of the programs that work for their personal needs and style.

These programs can also supplement and enhance the employer's retirement savings education programs, helping employees achieve financial wellness today and in the future.

Voluntary Debt and Credit Counseling programs help employees who are facing urgent debt and credit problems, providing helpful tools and resources.

Debt and credit are widespread problems for today's workforce. Employees coming into the workforce are often faced with massive amounts of college debt that must be repaid.

And there is a growing number of employed individuals who have poor credit ratings and significant credit card debt.

Employers can offer voluntary programs that help employees manage their debt and credit. Counseling, credit monitoring and reporting, credit restoration services, credit card and debt management, budgeting and help with bankruptcies and foreclosures is available. Help with understanding and improving credit scores is also offered.

Available programs include one-on-one counseling and web-based personal finance calculation and modeling tools, including on-line learning centers.

When employees get help and pay off their loans and debts, they can then be encouraged to keep making payments as payroll deductions for employee benefits.

Voluntary Product Purchasing Plans

Product purchasing programs help employees buy what they need in a responsible way and pay through payroll deductions. These programs are popular with employees who want to make payments over time. They generally offer access to recognized brands at competitive prices.

Spending limits based on the employees' salary levels are inherent in the program design, protecting them from overextending on purchases.

Products for purchase typically available through these programs include electronics, computers, household appliances, furniture, fitness equipment and more. Recent product purchasing plan innovations include vacation travel and college tuition.

People with cash and/or good credit can go into a store or go on-line and buy products easily and at reasonable prices. Others may only be able to make a purchase using credit at a high interest rate. For an employee whose refrigerator breaks down and is not repairable, a product purchasing plan may be a very attractive answer to an immediate household crisis!

Another benefit to these plans is that employees get used to the payroll deduction. When the product is paid in full, this is another opportunity to encourage employees to continue the deduction, paying for another needed Voluntary Benefit or contributing towards their retirement savings.

Congratulations! Together we have surveyed 21 of the very best Voluntary Benefits. Here's the list of all 21 Voluntary Benefits:

21 Voluntary Benefits

1. **Critical Illness**
2. **Dental**
3. **Vision**
4. **Hearing**
5. **Health Wellness**
6. **Hospitalization**
7. **Accident**
8. **Telemedicine**
9. **Life Insurance**
10. **Short Term Disability**
11. **Long Term Disability**
12. **Long Term Care**
13. **Legal Services**
14. **Identity Theft Protection**
15. **Auto Insurance**
16. **Home Insurance**
17. **Pet Protection/Insurance**
18. **Child and Elder Care**
19. **Financial Education and Counseling**
20. **Debt and Credit Counseling**
21. **Product Purchasing**

Your Voluntary Benefits Tool Kit. Part 1 of our Guide showed you the 21 Voluntary Benefits that your employees want and will appreciate you for offering.

The next two Parts of our Guide are a tool kit filled with actionable ideas and techniques to help you build or expand your Voluntary Benefits Program.

PART 2

7 Keys to Voluntary Benefits

Now that you've explored the Voluntary Benefits available today and have identified those you want to add to your benefits program, you're ready to take the actions needed to introduce the new Voluntary Benefits to your employees. This Part 2 of our Guide highlights seven key processes and concepts which will help you successfully launch your expanded Voluntary Benefits program.

Begin with a strategic benefits inventory, consider affordability and payroll convenience, plan your enrollment calendar, communicate, recognize the importance of Voluntary Benefits to women and join with your vendor partners. These are seven keys to Voluntary Benefits success!

7 Keys to Voluntary Benefits

1. **Benefits Inventory**
2. **Affordability**
3. **Payroll Convenience**
4. **Enrollment**
5. **Communication**

73

6. **Voluntary Benefits for Women**
7. **Vendor Business Partners**

Chapter 6

Key #1 – Voluntary Benefits Inventory

Key #1 – Voluntary Benefits Inventory. Create a strategic inventory of the Voluntary Benefits that are featured in your program today, and identify program gaps. Consider expanding your inventory to include all your benefits and compensation programs to help you identify how and where Voluntary Benefits fit in your Total Rewards/Compensation strategy.

An inventory is a helpful tool to manage your benefits program. It can be used for planning and designing your program. It can be used to communicate your program to new and current employees and to your senior management. And it can be used as a tool when working with your brokers/consultants. It can be a list, a spreadsheet, or whatever form works for you and your company.

We've published a comprehensive strategic inventory tool that we call the Managing Benefits Strategic Inventory™ (available as a bonus gift to you from the authors – download it at the Bonus Resources page). You may want to use this tool to help you prepare your dynamic benefits inventory – one that is regularly reviewed and evaluated. Many employers have never put down in one place all the benefits they offer, let alone all the total rewards they provide to their employees. Regardless of whether an employer adopts a total rewards concept, this inventory can be helpful because it creates a tool the employer can use strategically.

As you build your inventory, think about the life needs of your employees, and the programs that help them meet these needs. Then review the growing menu of Voluntary Benefits that are available to meet each of those needs.

Chapter 7

Key #2 – Affordability

Key #2 – Affordability. As you consider offering Voluntary Benefits to your employees, help them understand the impact on their total payroll deductions. Affordability depends on the balance between their life needs and the cost of the plan - measured by the impact on their take-home pay. Help employees to identify the coverages they need and to determine whether the Voluntary Benefits plans offered by your company meet these needs.

Employers continue to move towards more shared responsibility between the employer and the employee for the costs of all benefits. The trend towards a defined contribution approach for core programs is growing. The total amount of deductions for benefits from an employee's paycheck is becoming an important strategic consideration for benefits design. At stake is the effectiveness of benefits as an attraction and retention tool.

The employee's share of the total cost of benefits plans is increasing. Defined contribution retirement plans are designed to encourage significant payroll based contributions towards the employee's retirement security. Health plan designs are increasing the employee's share of the total cost of services and the payroll deducted "premium" continues to increase. It's in this context that an employee is making the decision to choose deductions for Voluntary Benefits. Some contributions to benefits plans are tax advantaged, and this can be an important factor impacting the overall employee willingness to spend on benefits.

In evaluating the employee cost for Voluntary Benefits, the discussion is often framed in terms of the affordability of the voluntary program being considered, and affordability is often evaluated separately for each plan. But for employers, it's important to recognize that employees look at their take home pay after all the deductions are taken for benefits. The better analysis for the employee is to first understand what coverages and protections are available and needed under the Voluntary Benefits program for that employee's individual and family circumstances. Once that needs analysis is understood, then deductions, which when looked at in isolation may seem challenging, may be recognized by the employee as money well spent. Each employee needs to have his or her own personal strategic benefits plan!

Chapter 8

Key #3 – Payroll Convenience

Key #3 – Payroll Convenience. Voluntary Benefits offered through the workplace feature convenient payroll deductions that result in regular deductions each pay period. These are often more manageable for employees than one-time direct billed premiums, and their personal budgeting may be simplified.

Employees appreciate the convenience of regular and automatic payroll deductions, eliminating the need for periodic billing and payments. For example, auto and home insurance when purchased directly as a consumer is generally billed annually or semi-annually. In contrast to these large one time payments, auto and home insurance voluntary programs set up regular payments spread over the year which are automatically deducted form an employee's paycheck. This helps employees budget throughout the year, and is an added convenience for them.

As an alternative to payroll deduction, some plans offer employees direct billing or automatic bank account debit arrangements.

Providers prefer receiving regular streams of premium payments that are administratively consolidated. This enables the providers to offer the voluntary coverage at a more favorable rate when compared to the individual market. The result for the employer is that important life needs of employees are being met and the more favorable rates are appreciated by their employees.

Chapter 9

Key #4 – Enrollment

Key #4 – Enrolling in Voluntary Benefits - Your Benefits Calendar. Be sure that your employees know the enrollment rules and dates for your Voluntary Benefits. Their ability to participate in the Voluntary Benefits you offer depends on each plan's enrollment rules and the dates that the plan is offered. Be sure employees know whether there will be an "open enrollment" period and that they know the eligibility rules and how they differ if the employee enrolls during the "open enrollment" period or if they enroll later. Many Voluntary Benefits can be offered and enrolled "off-cycle" – any time during the year.

The benefits calendar for core benefits is overwhelmingly driven by the annual enrollment cycle for health care benefits. When health care enrollment is offered in the fall, employers frequently take the opportunity to communicate not only health care, but also to encourage retirement savings. Employees are urged to evaluate whether their other choices for benefits are appropriate to their current individual and family circumstances. Employers often use this opportunity to remind employees to review their life insurance and disability coverages and update their beneficiary designations.

Many employers also use their open enrollment communications to remind employees of their Voluntary Benefits choices. Taken together, this amount of employee benefits communication at one time can be overwhelming to employees. We know that employees typically spend only a few minutes each year making their benefits choices, relying very often on a default election which continues their current benefits elections. Effective and frequent communication can help employees make these important benefits decisions.

Voluntary Benefits that complement core benefits offerings are best communicated during the annual enrollment period. For example, when an employee is deciding whether to participate in a high deductible health plan, the availability of critical illness and hospitalization coverage on a voluntary basis can play an important role. And employees should consider supplemental life insurance when you remind them of their basic life insurance coverage.

Other Voluntary Benefits are not tied to the annual benefits enrollment cycle. They can be offered and chosen at any time during the year. These benefits have no qualifying events as a condition to enrollment, and are not tied to a specific time of the year. For example, an employee's personal auto and home insurance policies can renew at any time during a calendar year, and it's at that time that they are most likely to consider enrolling in the employer's Voluntary Benefits program. Product purchasing programs, pet insurance, identity theft and legal services plans are other examples of Voluntary Benefits that can be offered at any time during the year.

Plan vendors support enrollment campaigns for Voluntary Benefits, both when the benefit is first

---

introduced and then in subsequent years. Off cycle eligibility may be attractive to employers because it gives the employer the opportunity to communicate the value of their benefits program any time during the calendar year (and often), not just once at open enrollment.

Some Voluntary Benefits have underwriting requirements. If the underwriting requirements are waived or are otherwise more favorable when the benefit is first introduced, it may be preferable to have the initial introduction separate from your health care enrollment in order to focus employee attention on the unique opportunity to take advantage of the favorable underwriting.

You can select the type of Voluntary Benefits enrollment process offered to your employees, taking into account your culture, history of enrollment, and workforce and employer preferences. Enrollment can be in person – one-on-one or group meetings - and with or without the support of a call center.

Vendor platforms may offer a menu of benefits choices where enrollment is frequently completed on-line, using video and interactive avatars to help employees better understand the choices available to them. Some employers prefer to use paper enrollment and email or direct mail – generally to the home so that family members can be involved in coverage decisions. You can also use a combination of enrollment vehicles.

Whatever method you use, use it also as an opportunity to communicate your entire benefits program. (See Key#5 – Communication)

While there is a focus on enrollment activities when a plan is first introduced, it's equally important to have a process for providing information about the plans to new employees as part of their onboarding. And employees who have had a life event should be offered the opportunity to review all the benefits that may be available to them which may be appropriate for their new life status.

When evaluating the benefits for a job at a new company, new hires will be looking at the total benefits offered by the employer. Be sure that the Voluntary Benefits your company offers are described in your recruiting material.

Voluntary Benefits are often "portable". This means that former employees can continue participating in the plan and pay the plan directly. Communications to your terminating employees should describe the portability features and plan rules for continuing to participate in the program, and contacts for further information about continued participation.

We encourage employers to develop what we call the Managing Benefits Calendar™. You can use this special calendar to implement your strategic benefits plan throughout the year – for both your core and Voluntary Benefits. (A one page blueprint for your Managing Benefits Calendar™ is available to download on the Bonus Resources page of this Guide.)

Chapter 10

Key #5 – Communication

Key #5 – Communicate – Communicate – Communicate. Voluntary Benefits provide unique opportunities to communicate the value of your entire benefits program. At the same time as you communicate your Voluntary Benefits, you can deliver strong messages that demonstrate the value of your core health, retirement and basic financial protection benefits. Take advantage of the many recent innovations in benefits communication – including on-line, mobile and social media.

Effective communication is critical to achieving a successful benefits program. Employees need to better understand their benefits, and strong communication can increase your employees' appreciation of the value the benefits your company makes available. Benefits messages must be visible and easily understood. Communication should be frequent; periodic communication throughout the year is desirable to increase the visibility and perceived value of your program.

Employees need to know why Voluntary Benefits coverage is important. They need tools to help them determine how plans will help them meet their life needs, the cost of the plans and the impact of payroll deductions on their take home pay. And of course they must have sufficient information to help them understand not only what the plans cover, but also what they don't. As we saw in the discussion on enrollment, there are many vehicles for communicating Voluntary Benefits, and the timing of information about some of these plans can be "off-cycle", separate from annual open enrollment activities.

Voluntary Benefits communication can enhance the communication of your core benefits and address individual needs. Communicating Voluntary Benefits throughout the calendar year increases employee appreciation and understanding of your entire benefits program. Use these opportunities to present your full benefits program and emphasize how the different plans relate to each other, and the life needs they may meet.

Voluntary Benefits vendors will often support communication of your entire benefits program when presenting their products.

When communicating Voluntary Benefits consider the generational differences in your workforce. Explore the feasibility of grouping benefits together to present multi-plan packages appropriate to meet different generational needs.

Chapter 11

Key #6 – Voluntary Benefits for Women

Key #6 – Voluntary Benefits for Women. Women – whether they are sole or primary breadwinners, part of a 2-income family or the spouses/partners of your employees – have significant needs for the financial protections and financial well-being resources that Voluntary Benefits offer. To meet their unique needs you'll want to explore innovative ways to communicate Voluntary Benefits to women in your workforce.

Voluntary Benefits are especially important to help women meet their needs for financial protection. Frequently, women are underinsured for life insurance and disability coverage and it's important for them to know what your company offers and how to best take advantage of these resources.

Voluntary Benefits not only promote the financial well-being of women in the workforce; these benefits also improve business productivity and help make your company a best place to work for women. Work with your broker/consultant or plan provider to develop focused communications to help women employees understand the financial value of all their benefits. Highlight the advantages of Voluntary Benefits for women and their families – favorable group premiums, portability, convenience of payroll deductions, and the ability to choose options tailored to meet their individual needs.

Chapter 12

Key #7 – Vendor Business Partners

Key #7 – Teaming with your Voluntary Benefits vendors – including brokers/consultants, product providers and administration specialists, and now private benefits exchanges – is key to the successful introduction and ongoing implementation of Voluntary Benefits. Your external vendor team will provide many of the communication, enrollment, administration and other resources you need.

You want your vendors to provide you with regular updates and briefings on current and new products, services, administration tools, and trends in Voluntary Benefits. You want them to be familiar with your full benefits program and to understand where their Voluntary Benefits plans fit in.

Your broker/consultant fulfills a variety of important roles in support of your Voluntary Benefits program. They provide an overview of the products, providers, services and innovations in the Voluntary Benefits market. They help you identify the best fit for your company and your employees. They are key to coordinating the components of a successful Voluntary Benefits program.

As well as offering a wide range of Voluntary Benefits products, insurance companies and other Voluntary Benefits providers also supply support for communication, enrollment and administration.

Many of these providers bring extensive experience in the retail product and core employee benefits markets. Providers of core health, life and disability employee benefits often now have coordinated product offerings, combining core benefits and complementary Voluntary Benefits. For example, some health insurers now offer critical illness and hospitalization Voluntary Benefits along with their medical plan products.

Voluntary Benefits providers are introducing product innovations designed to meet the growing demand for Voluntary Benefits from employers looking to strengthen their benefits programs without incurring additional direct costs.

Vendors who deliver services supporting enrollment and ongoing administration are vital to making your Voluntary Benefits program successful. They help your HR/Benefits departments, which are already stretched thin, to both manage and administer your Voluntary Benefits program.

Innovations in recordkeeping platforms provide payroll integration and support for communication, enrollment and administration, relieving you of many of these burdens.

Accurate, flawless administration of all benefits is critical to employee appreciation and plan governance. When you introduce a new Voluntary Benefit you want to be sure that processes are in place to effectively administer the plan. Payroll deductions must accurately reflect the employee's election and be processed quickly once the election is made. Data reflecting the employee's election and the payroll deducted premium must be sent to the provider in time for coverage to start on schedule. These processes may be supported by payroll integration tools supplied by either the plan provider or a third party. Often benefits consultants and brokers will have tools available to facilitate these processes.

The emergence and prominence of benefits administration platforms has had a significant impact on the administration of traditional benefits programs and promises to be even more important as a solution enabling employers to readily offer a full menu of Voluntary Benefits. The new platforms address not only the administrative interfaces needed between the employer payroll function and the carriers, but also include innovative enrollment, communication and education tools that support and enhance employee understanding of Voluntary Benefits choices. The platforms deliver technology solutions frequently supported by call centers and on-site enrollers.

Private Benefits Exchanges. The introduction of private benefits exchanges with the corresponding creation of benefits marketplaces has created more choices for employers. Originally focused on health products, many private exchanges now incorporate Voluntary Benefits. You'll see Voluntary Benefits included on the menu of benefits and fully coordinated with core benefits enrollment decisions. When employers use a Defined Contribution approach to their benefits, employees can apply those contributions to both core and voluntary products.

As with health plans offered on many exchanges where multiple vendors and different plan options/levels are available, competing Voluntary Benefits plans and different product vendors can also be made available to employees.

The exchanges facilitate administration for both health plans and Voluntary Benefits. The enrollment process becomes a one-stop shopping experience for your employees, with strong communications and decision support tools available.

Today, as an employer, you want to be well versed on the advantages and challenges of moving to a private exchange. The forms of exchanges and the players in the market are rapidly evolving. Senior management is reading about these exchanges and about Voluntary Benefits. They'll want to be regularly updated on these major employee benefits trends.

Here are the seven keys you can use to unlock the potential of Voluntary Benefits for your employees.

7 Keys to Voluntary Benefits

1. **Benefits Inventory**
2. **Affordability**
3. **Payroll Convenience**
4. **Enrollment**
5. **Communication**
6. **Voluntary Benefits for Women**
7. **Vendor Business Partners**

* * * * * * * * * * * * * *

In the third and final Part of our Guide, we'll take you through a checklist for getting started on your first – or next – Voluntary Benefits.

PART 3

10 Quick Steps to Voluntary Benefits Success:

A Managing Benefits™ Checklist

Benefits aren't simple. You don't just push a button or hit "Enter" to add new Voluntary Benefits. The reality is that introducing any employee benefits plan is a complex challenge.

We've developed a 10-step checklist for putting in Voluntary Benefits. It's your recipe for success!

We like checklists. (See our Note on Checklists.) When we coach employee benefits pros, using our Managing Benefits System™, we emphasize the power of checklists to help focus on the steps that are most critical to benefits program success.

Starting from scratch? Or already have some Voluntary Benefits in place for your employees? Use this valuable checklist to manage the steps to introduce and run your new or enhanced Voluntary Benefits program.

Here are 10 quick steps for putting it all together.

Your 10 Step Checklist

1. **Start, Look and Listen**
2. **Selection and Design**
3. **Resources**
4. **Select Your Product Provider**
5. **Build Your Vendor Team**
6. **Launch Date**
7. **Your Introduction/ Implementation Schedule**
8. **Launch**
9. **Review Success**
10. **Next Steps**

Chapter 13

Strategy, Design and Resources

Checklist Step #1 – Start, Look and Listen

Review the 21 Voluntary Benefits highlighted in this Guide. Identify your possible programs. What peaks your interest? What are your employees telling you? What are you hearing from your broker/consultant? From other employers? From your current benefits providers?

Checklist Step #2 – Selection and Design

Identify your top Voluntary Benefits candidates to add to your benefits program. Be sure that the plans you've identified fit with your benefits strategy. How do they complement your current benefits program? Use input generated by your Benefits Inventory (see Key #1 – Voluntary Benefits Inventory). Many categories of Voluntary Benefits present design choices. Finalize your selections and make your major design decisions.

Checklist Step #3 – Resources

Identify the resources available to help you. Talk to your broker/consultant. Discuss the Voluntary Benefits you've chosen with your current product vendors – these vendors may offer some or all of the new plans you're considering. Early on, you'll want to involve others on your management team whose support will be important to the ultimate success of your new Voluntary Benefits. Your internal team will depend on the size and resources of your organization. In addition to HR/Benefits, your team may include your financial/controllers/treasurer group, payroll department, legal counsel (for regulatory and tax compliance), purchasing, technology and communications. Your team's input will help refine the design of each new program. Each team member will be ready to contribute their expertise and resources as you implement the new benefits.

Chapter 14

Provider, Product and Team Selection

Checklist Step #4 – Select Your Product Providers

Now that you've decided which benefits you're going to introduce and you've gathered product design and provider information (including their qualifications), you'll want to obtain proposals from one or more of the product providers. You may want to do a full RFP, or you may choose to ask for sales proposals. You and your internal team will evaluate the proposals, which will describe not only plan design and costs, but also support and administrative services.

Based on the proposals, you may be ready to make your selection, or you may want to arrange for presentations by the finalists. During these presentations, you'll be able to evaluate, face-to-face, the provider team that will be working with your company.

The information you gather will enable you to select the best product providers to support your new Voluntary Benefits

Checklist Step #5 – Build Your Vendor Team

Your vendor team consists of not only product providers.

Your broker/consultant plays an integral part in achieving success – often quarterbacking the entire selection and implementation process.

Your broker/consultant and your product providers will identify other needed members of the team, who may be within their organizations or from companies they partner with for product implementations. If you're using a private exchange for benefits, many of these vendor tasks are integrated into the exchange.

The team may include a professional enrollment firm and a communication specialist, as well as a benefits administration platform provider. Be sure your vendor team matches the needs of your organization and evaluate the support that the vendors can provide. Be sure you understand the cost of each vendor's services and how they are compensated.

Chapter 15

Schedule and Launch

Checklist Step #6 – Launch Date

The launch date of the new Voluntary Benefits should be coordinated with the rest of your Benefits Calendar. Some employers choose to link the enrollment of all benefits plans to their annual enrollment. Other employers may choose an off-cycle separate enrollment period, spreading "benefits news" throughout the year.

When choosing the target introduction date that's right for your company, recognize that some Voluntary Benefits may offer enrollment throughout the year, following an initial introductory campaign.

Once you've established a target enrollment date, develop your Introduction/Implementation Schedule to meet that target.

Checklist Step #7 – Your Introduction/Implementation Schedule

Depending on factors such as your company's size, complexity, workforce locations, and internal systems, your Introduction/Implementation Schedule could be as short as a couple of months or as long as a year. Your internal and external teams will be critical to developing your timeline. Be sure your vendors and internal resources can accommodate each step.

Identify the components of your Introduction/Implementation Schedule, and the timing for each element. Brainstorm with your teams to develop a workable schedule, culminating with the launch date.

You'll want your schedule to take into account all key factors, including, deliverables to employees, administration and communication.

Using a spreadsheet or your company's preferred project planning tools, develop a project plan for your Introduction/Implementation Schedule.

Checklist Step #8 – Launch

Now that you've developed your project plan, you're ready to launch.

You want your administration systems to be ready for testing no less than a month before the date the new benefits become effective (the "launch date"). Your payroll and your benefits administration platforms and the vendor interfaces that support the programs must be set up so that contributions are deducted correctly and benefits elections are communicated to the provider on a timely basis.

The call center supporting your enrollment activities needs to be up and running at least 2 weeks before the enrollment period begins. Representatives need to be trained not only in the new program but also the systems that support it.

Whether you're using an established platform such as a private exchange or a carrier's voluntary benefits platform or a third party benefits administration tool, the web based tools and any mobile apps must be tested to ensure that they reflect your program and your intended employee experience.

While your administrative systems are being developed and tested, you'll be working with the plan providers and your brokers/consultants to prepare the education, announcement and enrollment materials for your employees.

Once you announce the program, your focus will be on communication, enrollment and administration. The announcement should be scheduled at least 4 weeks before the launch date.

Here's a *sample* schedule for the weeks leading to the launch date of a new plan.

At least 4 weeks before the launch date, you'll begin communications and enrollment. Phone, web and app based chat facilities will be in place for employee questions. Communications can be online or in print, including announcements, plan summaries, enrollment forms and descriptions and benefits newsletters. Communications can also include benefits fairs, employee meetings, videos, podcasts, apps and social media tools. Employees may make enrollment elections online or meeting face-to-face with enrollment specialists.

At 3 weeks to launch date, follow-up reminders are sent. Note that enrollment may involve connecting the employee with an agent who will work directly with them. Auto and Home insurance plans and Long Term Care are examples of programs where the vendor agents may have ongoing discussions with interested employees.

Two weeks before the launch date, enrollment ends. Elections are reported to payroll, product vendors, etc., as needed.

One week before the launch date, confirmation of enrollment is sent to employees, including any results from those plans with underwriting requirements.

Congratulations!! Your new Voluntary Benefits are launched! Plan coverage becomes effective and payroll deductions begin as of the launch date.

Chapter 16

Review and Repeat

Checklist Step #9 – Review Success

Now that your program is up and running, you have the results of the enrollment. It's a good time to review your program success.

The most common measurement is the enrollment percentage. How many employees took advantage of each offering? Other measures include employee feedback – both on the Voluntary Benefits offered and the process.

Were the plan designs that were offered the right ones for your employee population? Was the communication campaign successful? Did your employees understand the value of the benefit? Did the enrollment process go smoothly?

What did you hear from your employees? Are they aware that the plans were available at your company?

Successful enrollment percentages vary with the type of plan offered. Your broker/consultant and plan provider have data that you can compare with your results. Be sure that the data you're looking at is comparable to your employee population and company demographics.

While the initial enrollment results are very important, don't lose sight of the longer term view. Over time, you want enrollment to increase. You also want to measure the "lapse rate", to be comfortable that your employees are continuing to value and participate in the plans.

Checklist Step #10 – Next Steps

Continue to monitor the ongoing administration of the plans. Identify processes for new hires. How are you communicating to new hires? Is your enrollment process working for your new hires?

Prepare annual reminders to current employees. Address the needs of employees who have family status or other life changes, ensuring that they have the opportunity to make revised elections suitable for their circumstances.

Use employee and vendor feedback and your enrollment results to plan for your next introduction of new Voluntary Benefits.

Remember to communicate with terminating employees as well so that they can take advantage of portability opportunities.

The introduction of Voluntary Benefits is a long term process with the ultimate goal of offering a wide range of benefits to fully address the diverse needs of your workforce. You'll want to review the menu of Voluntary Benefits available in the marketplace and continue to enhance your benefits program. Remember, there are at least 21 Voluntary Benefits we are sure employees will love!

Remember to use this Checklist whenever you are adding Voluntary Benefits to your benefits program.

10 Quick Steps to Voluntary Benefits Success:

A Managing Benefits™ Checklist

1.	**Start, Look and Listen**
2.	**Selection and Design**
3.	**Resources**
4.	**Select Your Product Provider**
5.	**Build Your Vendor Team**
6.	**Launch Date**
7.	**Your Introduction/ Implementation Schedule**
8.	**Launch**
9.	**Review Success**
10.	**Next Steps**

* * * * * * * * * * * * * *

Now you have everything you need to get started and to cross the finish line – 21 Voluntary Benefits to offer, 7 key best practices and 10 quick steps you can start today!

Chapter 17

Afterword

We've devoted our professional careers to employee benefits, convinced that quality benefits programs are both good business and good for employees and their families.

When Donna speaks to HR and Benefits Pro's at conferences she always tells them that she is *passionate* about employee benefits. We hope that we have demonstrated our enthusiasm in this book.

We hope employers will join in, enhancing the value of their employee benefits programs through greatly expanded use of Voluntary Benefits.

As a successful employer you have done an amazing job over the past few years - navigating the challenging worlds of competition, new generations of employees, economic crisis and recovery, and major legislation, combined with rapid changes in technology and communication. You continue to recognize that it's possible to enhance your employee benefits program to better attract and retain the best and most productive talent, and to better meet the life needs of your employees. This book provides a roadmap for achieving that potential. Voluntary Benefits, when added to your benefits mix, makes the possible become reality in your business.

Employers offering a menu of Voluntary Benefits help employees readily find plans which meet life needs. Employees with Voluntary Benefits choices at work are not left on their own researching answers to the stressful challenges of their complex lives.

Most employers recognize the need for core health, retirement, and financial protection benefits. But their benefits programs today must, of necessity, reflect the realities of their business' ability to support the cost of benefits. The multiple generations in today's workforce are best served when they have options to choose from – for both core and Voluntary Benefits. As we say, "Voluntary Benefits are the Benefits You Choose"™ – for both employers and employees.

Voluntary benefits can propel every employer's benefits program to realize its full potential for business success and satisfy the full range of life needs of employees and their families.

It's no longer a question of whether each and every employer will offer a comprehensive suite of Voluntary Benefits – it's only a question of when.

Use this book as your personal guide to getting started and quickly moving forward to establish or enhance your Voluntary Benefits program.

Please be sure to share with us your successes and challenges as you embark on, or renew, your Voluntary Benefits journey.

Thank you for reading our book.

Donna Joseph   Pete Tobiason

Bonus Resources

Managing Benefits Strategic Inventory™

For help in developing your Voluntary Benefits Inventory (KEY #1 in Chapter 6), download our complimentary Managing Benefits Strategic Inventory™, a tool which identifies the variety of programs that make up today's Total Rewards. To download your copy, go to **www.RJTAdvisors.com/resources**.

Managing Benefits Plan Key™ for Voluntary Benefits

For an action-oriented one-page tool outlining the actions, team members and stakeholders in your Voluntary Benefits program, download our complimentary Managing Benefits Plan Key™ for Voluntary Benefits. To download your copy, go to **www.RJTAdvisors.com/resources**

Managing Benefits Calendar™

For a complimentary blueprint to use in setting up your own Managing Benefits Calendar™ (KEY #4 in Chapter 9), go to **www.RJTAdvisors.com/resources**.

Newsletters

Sign up for our email periodic news and updates on employee benefits. To sign up for our newsletters, go to **http://bit.ly/RJTANews**

Acknowledgements

We want to acknowledge the help given us by our many friends in the Voluntary Benefits community. Their continuing support has helped us to better understand and write about the dramatic recent development of the Voluntary Benefits marketplace.

We thank Walt Podgurski, for recognizing early in our coaching and consulting journey that we have a Voluntary Benefits message vital to both employers and brokers/consultants.

Special thanks to Mark Parabicoli and Rob DeFrancisco and to other key players at Voluntary Benefits product and service providers who support our employer focused approach to Voluntary Benefits. Thank you to Brian Bellows, Nick Cianci, Ross Linthicum, Mark Roberts, Jan Soppe and Peter Toth.

For all benefits, communication is key to success. Jennifer Benz has been a valued friend and colleague, bringing innovative ideas to delivering benefits messages to employees.

We thank Ken Sperling, Chris Condeluci and Sherri Bockhorst for their insights into the rapidly developing private exchange landscape.

For help understanding the special role Voluntary Benefits can play to help women's financial well-being we thank Cindy Hounsell of Wiser Women.

Many others who work in Voluntary Benefits have helped us and to all, we say a heartfelt thanks.

We also want to acknowledge and thank our former ITT colleagues, corporate benefits leaders and the benefits and legal advisors that we were fortunate to work with during our corporate careers - too many to mention individually. Whether it was developing our benefits philosophy, strategizing, designing programs, implementing plans, and ongoing benefits plan management to ensure the program was administered in the best interests of employees, retirees and the company or teaming for the many acquisitions and other transactions we completed - we were surrounded by intelligent and practical colleagues, advisors and product providers.

Thank you always to our longtime friends and colleagues, Craig Rosenthal and Debbie Schmieder.

We are thankful for the support and friendship of all those we worked with at ABC (the American Benefits Council) and ERIC (the ERISA Industry Committee), as well as other employer groups.

We especially thank our good friend Jim Klein for his counsel and encouragement as we grew our new company.

And of course, we both are so very grateful for our families and thank them for all their support and encouragement as we developed and wrote this Guide.

About the Authors

Donna Joseph is the CEO and co-founder of Rhodes-Joseph & Tobiason Advisors, an independent, woman-owned employee benefits coaching company helping employers and HR and Employee Benefits professionals, as well as brokers/consultants, vendors and service providers, **www.RJTAdvisors.com**. Donna leads her company's Grow Your Benefits Career™ coaching practice, **www.GrowYourBenefitsCareer.com**.

As former Benefits Director at a major global company and former Board member of ABC, the American Benefits Council, Donna brings her wide experience, depth of knowledge and employer perspective to her clients.

She frequently speaks at major HR and Employee Benefits conferences, including the SHRM Annual Conference, Employee Benefits Forum & Expo, Human Resource Executive Health & Benefits Leadership Conference, Employer HealthCare Congress, Benefits Selling Expo, and Workplace Benefits Renaissance and Mania.

Follow Donna on Twitter (@BenefitsCoach) and connect on LinkedIn.

Pete Tobiason is an Employee Benefits Professional, Coach, Author and Speaker with more than 30 years experience in employee benefits leadership, management, training, speaking, and coaching. A former Employee Benefits Counsel at a major global company and former Chair of ERIC, the ERISA Industry Committee, he coaches HR and benefits professionals and businesses on managing benefits. He is President and co-founder of Rhodes-Joseph & Tobiason Advisors, the Managing Benefits™ Coaching Company, **www.RJTAdvisors.com** and is a Principal in the firm's Grow Your Benefits Career™ coaching practice,

www.GrowYourBenefitsCareer.com

He and the firm's CEO and co-founder, Donna Joseph, deliver value to their clients through creative and innovative solutions to employee benefits challenges, bringing experienced and independent employer perspective.

Follow Pete on Twitter (@PeteRJTA) and connect on LinkedIn.

Donna and Pete co-authored the eBook *Making Voluntary Workplace Benefits Part of Every Employer's Benefits Program*, a guide helping brokers/consultants and benefits product providers understand the employer's perspective on employee benefits.

Managing Benefits™

Our employee benefits strategic leadership and management system and products, services and publications that help transform benefits programs and benefits professionals' careers using an integrated system of tools and techniques for managing employee benefits.

Note on Checklists

Experts tell us that one of the best ways to manage in high risk situations and avoid costly mistakes is to use a checklist. This seemingly simple tool has been shown to reduce medical errors in hospitals by some 50% and pilots don't take off without reviewing their pre-flight checklist.

We recommend Atul Gawande's book, *The Checklist Manifesto: How to Get Things Right*, which documents the power of checklists. We've included a checklist in Part 3 of this Guide to help you manage your Voluntary Benefits program. After reading Atul Gawande's book, we hope you'll want to follow our checklist's 10 steps to a successful Voluntary Benefits program.

Coaching, Workshop and Speaking Services

Looking for more help with Voluntary Benefits or any other Benefits opportunity or challenge? Donna Joseph and Pete Tobiason are passionate about sharing with you their Employee Benefits ideas and experience.

Coaching

Donna Joseph and Pete Tobiason coach HR and Benefits Pros, Businesses and Benefits Brokers/Consultants and Benefits Products and Service Providers.

Visit **www.GrowYourBenefitsCareer.com**

Managing Benefits™ Leadership Workshops

Spend a day with Donna Joseph and Pete Tobiason at a small group intensive workshop. Learn how to lead and manage a successful, state-of-the-art Employee Benefits program, with in-depth training in our Managing Benefits System™. Visit **www.RJTAdvisors.com**

Speaking Services

Donna Joseph and Pete Tobiason are available for speaking events. Along with Voluntary Benefits, speaking topics include benefits leadership and management and benefits career development for HR and Benefits Pros. Email the authors at **info@RJTAdvisors.com**

Thank you for buying this Book

Published by Bayne & Prospect Books
an imprint of
Rhodes-Joseph & Tobiason Advisors

To receive special offers,
bonus content and news about employee
benefits
and our latest books, sign up for our
newsletter

bit.ly/RJTANews
(this address is case sensitive)

Or visit us online to sign up at

www.RJTAdvisors.com

Thank You for Reading

We hope you enjoyed reading *Employer's Quick Guide to 21 Voluntary Benefits* and are inspired to add Voluntary Benefits to your benefits program and that your employees will enjoy the rewards of having their life needs met by Voluntary Benefits. Or, if you are a broker/consultant or product or service provider, that you want your employer clients to better understand and appreciate today's Voluntary Benefits.

We would appreciate it if you left a review so employers who want to enhance their benefits program can profit from our ideas.

To better serve you, we'd like to know what you found helpful and what we can do to deliver even more value in the next edition.

If you have the time, you can post a review of this book on Amazon at **www.21VoluntaryBenefits.com**

Thank you so much for reading *21 Voluntary Benefits*.

With Gratitude,

Donna Joseph

Pete Tobiason